uncivilized

ecstasies

by happy oasis

for retail and wholesale book orders
please be in touch with *bliss u books* at:
www.blissologyuniversity.com/books
blissforth@blissologyuniversity.com
po box 2743 sedona, az 86339
ph 928.308.2146

galaxies of gratitude
to all adventurers
who live life fully in the
wilderness of the heart

in honor of

a kind old sage
of thirty-three or five
who amidst vast floods
in bangladesh
touched and smiled into the eyes
of each adult and starving child

i asked in tears,
"how can you smile?'
he said, "that's all i have to give"
then taught me to sing
to the withering
demonstrating how to live

dedication

speak such that thy words
are as sweet as is silence

moreover, may we write words worthy
of taking the lives of trees

are there such words?

uncivilized ecstasies
is dedicated to the
once-swaying trees
who are now
the pages
of this book

uncivilized

ecstasies

. . . and we sang from a scripture
from the belly of a rock
not a book
we sang visions through
our dancing fingers
never stopped
touching
the earth was all
we knew
sniffingtastinglisteningloving
the endless green womb of delight
where there was always
more than enough

long ago
before electricity
had entered the first box
electricity meant lightning bolt
the shimmering on a pond
your lover's touch
long ago
before the advent of
tvs and tractors
and even plows
before written religions
before the dusk of civilization
weird meant wonderful
living rooms were living
gospel signified god's spell
health meant whole meant holy
when invisible implied inwardly visible
we listened everywhere
and understood

your kisses tender as moss
cascade
then gather as pools
in forgotten recessed caverns
of my heart
let's build our home
in solitude together
a home with walls of freedom
and freely-shimmering trees
gables of sky
gentlekindness the foundation
beneath pastel breaths
and flutelike gazes
let's dream from the depths
of darkness darling
let's dream new dawns
how beautiful can they be?

what is rich?
one full day without cars
an evening without electricity
a meal without anyone
meddling with the food
is already perfect
sacred the way it is
why think nature's food
not good enough?
it *is* good enough
the sun has already baked it
as if the whole human world
has lost its gratitude
for the living miracle
called an apple
the exquisite bouquet of a carrot
or the soothing experience
of coconut nectar
entering inside you
attentively eating
conscious living beings
can feel eerie and tragic
yet inspiring
thus we pray not to a deity…

… we sing rather
to these plants before us
to these living fruit
and vegetable people
because everyone enjoys a song
especially when we are
about to be eaten
it seems the least one can do
we sing about the dance
of living and dying
and living again
by permeating everywhere
this is beautiful
this is important
this is the origin of prayer

we can destroy the legends of the sun
we can abandon the prayers
we can hide from the sky
in colossal boxes
and sleep long past every dawn
but the sun will still rise
to illuminate
to color
every aspect of creation
and shine
the sun will
shine upon even the most
dubious and dour
downtrodden and
industrial faces

thanks to these living vegetable people
we take nourishment
for super natural health
by inspiring deeply nature's verdure
sitting gratefully on the energizing earth
enjoying chewing each morsel
consuming slow fingerfuls wee and few
for those who eat little
live long
and vibrantly
this energy offered by your lives we vow to
use wisely by living gentle dynamic lives
we free ourselves from loitering
recklessly in buildings
honoring the inner whisper to abide in nature
we vow to emancipate ourselves from the
pandemic of materialism
by knowing when we have enough
and stopping
we prevent needless harm
and thus feel truly wealthy

you think i'm weird
i'm weirder than you think
you may think you understand me
we call this attempting to gather
all the wind beneath a single tree
at moments you may secretly claim
to know who this is
is only you
boo! over here

can we ever really know
a rainbow or two streams
of sunlight cloaked in skin?

what did I dream, dear?
i dreamt we were here
sleeping on this mountain
the winds ahowl
darkness everywhere
except for rare distant lights
far below and the vast expanse
of a universe ashimmer
we lay on our backs
above a steep and extensive wood
of pines on the summit of
this ancient volcano
we lay our bellies to the night sky
and slept quietly
without a single dream
of anywhere else

electricity does buzz
your room burns bright by light bulb
away where no bulbs burn
a timid candle flickers
when all the wax is spent
moon beams a sky-hung lantern
with nary a walker's moon
the universe is soon
our intimate relation
behold this cryptic room
by stellar illumination

hush

inhaling I appear
waltzing through trees
convening in crags
unfurling like silver spinnakers
without a whisper
i come
to wallow between the ribs of ridges
falling to the knees of peaks
drifting into dimples of sky
i am the mist
baptizer of trees
the water one who breathes
people into being
a feather, a wisp
the mother of clouds
i am the breath of dreams

what drug are you on
smirking first-world faces hack
is it acid, speed or smack

it's none of these yet so much more
i smile, i wink, inhale and snore

drugs of passage, paths of time
may fed our dreams, yet they're not mine

the sunrise is my lsd
kaleidoscopic ecstasy

daytime's clouds of pure cocaine
i infuse into each vein

each evening while inhaling paint
the sunset's acrid hellish taint

i sit aglow and wonder why
i'm hooked upon the trees and sky

i'd love to show you where I fly
 to holy cities with stones who cry…

... to sacred realms of fire and earth
retrieving our primordial birth

but you're satisfied with street-bought stuff
of only sticks of hash to puff

fooled by dealers advertising
you need crack, it's satisfying

when, I wonder, will we see
the high of highs is you is me

my hands still looked bloodstained
despite clouds which had rained
when i entered joey's shop
he knew just what I'd done
though i don't own a gun
he winked at me, nodded and stopped
without a breath more
he slammed shut the shop door
lest a customer in might drop
joey strode with a zoom
toward the shop's dark back room
you could hear him enter the freezer
he pulled back a drawer
fingered metal galore
thus equipped did reappear
i pulled out a hat lickety splat
brim with rubies from under my sweater
at the beauties he gasped
down we sat at long last
he pried open the container
we then both dug in, to feast to the skin
on wild berries and homemade ice cream
hush now that you know
that wild raspberries grow
by lush banks of the silverstone stream

we lookouts* are the hermits
of the 21st century
the sensitives and recluses
eccentrics without clear uses
seers akin to goddesses and dust
for we reside quietly inside
clouds overseeing creation
we, like goddesses and dust
are peaceful playful
and forgotten

* for ten gloriously refreshing, six-month long arizona
summers i abided on verdant volcanoes; upon aspen, fir,
maple and pine clad mountaintops between streams,
clouds, stars and dreams inside arizona's little known, high
altitude, seasonal rain and cloud forests while working for
the forest service as a "lookout", one who looks out for
fires from an isolated forest lookout tower and frequently
looks inside between recurrent visual sweeps of the vast
majestic accordions of mountains in all directions.

on the gathering of clouds

skyswimmer, our leader, said
we have to gather closer together
so we did
closer still, skyswimmer whispered
to make it happen
we moved like one long moment
wishing never to end
slowly drifting together
closer and closer
until our silver linings dissolved
when we became me
and i rained

gifts of gazing

alas! here we stand
touching hands together
everything is here everyone
we feel complete being near
nowhere to go
nothing to do
calmly abiding for this spell together
letting whatever arises arise
how ordinary how incredibly
extraordinarily ordinary
letting nectar flow between us
being entirely here
not having to run away
not having to move closer
or to hide behind words
or thought or deeds
just sharing a little infinity
inhaling an iota of sky
grateful for awkward moments

the fire started with hardly a flicker
just a distant glow which spread like
warm butter across
the whole of the horizon
all our forces, land and air
could not resist it
even up here in the lookout tower
the fire's blazing breath
commenced to heat the air
what an awesome sight
a vast broiling fire-exuding beast
this dance of sky-searing infernal splendor
imagine!
the sun was rising*

* in the wee hours of dawn
via our extensive shared radio network
an extremely elderly forest fire lookout
mistakenly reported this most unusual fire
and later that day decided it was about time to retire

mirabile dictu ~ wonderful to relate

be cautious while stepping
be gentle while sitting
be looking while leaning
know size is misleading

be sensing while stalking
be listening while talking
be conscious while dreaming
says scorpion* to me

*a surprising multitude of scorpions welcomed me and
offered wisdom during a silent month of solo hiking deep
inside the secret chasms of the grand canyon

25

tonight inside
guests boast of living
outside in the past
loquaciously refusing
tonight's "too icy" invitation
so you sit, you lookout, sit alone
above the canyon's sheer abode
with aspens and an owl
up there somewhere
beside this alpine fire

when the now is amply wild
tales of the past remain untold
spinning fables for what cause
is self-aggrandizement at large
when the self we share is grander
than imagination?

guests, we all are precious guests
come out, let's not forsake this night
stars blossom
ice clouds veil the sky
you stoke, woods wheeze
sparks firefly
spizzling invisible

along forgotten forest trails

bare feet
feeling strong
shirtless
i stride along
one cheek cool
one cheek warmed
by the rising sun

the question of inheriting your chair

dear dad,
when I was a child and you were away
i used to enter your den
remove the pile of papers from that old chair
wipe off the dust with the palm of my hand
and sit down deliberately
to dream
in that big old chair
which was your daughter's flying carpet
i would close my eyes
and feel the caress of polished wood
as if the chair were tenderly
carrying me back on its lap

soon i would hear the clopping of hooves
as brassy dust clouds rise above the road
behind bustling carriages
here's a gamboling girl in a calico dress
her hair braided with ribbons
her hands my hands
offering an apple from a basket
a blacksmith a peddler a farmer...

... walk past this window
tonight by flickering wood light

i'm now your grandfather whittle-listening
to the piano playing in the parlor
sitting in this chair
with quill and ink I write
a century past, this autumn night
as zephyrs snap leaves
to scatter in the sky

and on precious afternoons
(on that old chair, dad, in your den)
i would feel the chair coming alive
as a tree standing in the forest
revered by natives
at the ankle of a hill
birds flit across my shoulders of bark
breeze breathes through my leaves
sun is shining i am a tree content
now, dad, i no longer need
your grandfather's chair
(which secretly inherited me as a child)
i no longer need to close my eyes to see...

… today i live dipped in magic everywhere
here in the hush of dawn atop this peak
coyotes babble below
in unpeopled canyons
a rainbow rises from a hollow
a patient raven teaches me to caw
and deer emerge
from pinyon pine shadows
onto wild flowering slopes
of this volcano

once, an atlas was spun
and this question was hung:
lookouts, where is the ideal city?
we sighed with dismay
since not one could quite say
for there is no ideal city!
perhaps it is mirth, a meadow
or births of understanding
but it cannot be found
in the upturned ground
of buildings and concrete landings
it may be the shiver
of one's own hum quiver
serenading promenading vast silence
or the cool touch of mist
angelic wisps
gift-wrapping your bare abidance
from high up perched here
through a cloud may appear
the hint of a distant city
how trifling it seems
amidst stars trees and dreams
and like blessings from
nature's proximity

people are productive
busy busy building big houses
yet nature has already done it
busy busy investing and planting
while the wild and hardy grow
without human hands
busy busy driving clean cars
while forgoing the auto inside

forgetting yields needless toil
what did the shrubs do today?
what did the cliffs accomplish?
a lizard is absorbing sunshine
the sky is being the sky

all these years
and i've succeeded
at nothing in particular
just slumbering al fresco
dining on sunbeams and wild greens
and feeling perpetually amazed
by all of creation
true, I am healthy
and naturally quite glad
to have attained at middle age
nothing but liberation
to think or speak or neither
freedom to wander when one pleases
as swiftly or slowly as one wonders
and as delightedly

the birth of legends

with muddy feet
with pristine hearts
into a land of possibilities
they arrived
by arched foot bridges
joining churning river banks
they walked as if
through chinese paintings
with ricepaper parasols and scythes
humming tender somethings
back to the crooked trees
while listening to the waterfall song
of the fire-tailed birds
who are now called mythical

the prophet of profit
the god of gain
lets roam the thieves
in suits of plain
white collars with dollars
in sold out eyes
who grin as they spin
out well-groomed…. truths?

solitude
one stalks
on this peopled planet
silently
one walks
upon dark depths of granite
gratefully
one stands
basking asking nothing
marinating in creation

he embraces me with poetry
offering his-hands-picked peaches
tickling our elbows
with tongue-licked juice
we sing spontaneous songs
gorgeous songs gratefully gazing
twirling and honoring the dipping moon
sipping sweet silence we cherish this
prayer called stars and darkness
into the dawning
into the afternoon

breathing midstream
appeared this dream
a fancy, a realization
i'd like to be famous
not crowd-stage famous
but famous with my relations
i'd like to be famous with all i meet
and all to be famous with me
this fame feels more like affection
honor fondness affinity
imagine the whole world
famous together
celebrating what's special what's same
holding hearts dear
while connecting
this is the original fame

you come to witness the alpenglow
as i watch twilight rise in your eyes
you come to marvel at the heavens
while i see you a miracle
you come to dance together
yet i feel your dance is complete
you beseech me for a blessing
before you i bow

to abide on an alp is
to be rich with wind song
at ease in the society of trees
agog with the shimmering set on
silvering the raindrops of
tousled clouds
who will wander indoors
left open
sometimes huffing while rushing
to offer hail stones
other times lingering
for the afternoon
like a gentle friend

he said you are not grounded enough
inside we ask, are we heavenly enough?
who's to say?

if sleeping on the earth
eating from the earth
appreciating the earth
living with the earth
is not grounded enough
what is meant by grounded?

corpulent? mechanical?
trapped? conventional?
smitten by the pandemic of materialism?
deadened? hardened? glum?
may one be too grateful
blithe empty free?

inhaling the horizon
where earth meets sky
who is not both grounded and heavenly?

am i heavenly enough?
am i heavenly enough?
here lives our concern

black-eyed clouds overheard a raindance
sponsored by native flora
so flew from faraway mountains
to gather together to perform a storm

"give me spring!" teetered a thirsty tree
up to a dragon-edged cloud
who blinked with lightning and began
bepuddling and refloodling
the wash in thundering procession

the desert soon swam in coffee-silt streams
an ancient tree teetered in waves of foam
gulped from the sky a grumble a moan
then so slowly fell thunder-rumbling
as if echoing the storm

how to access the divine?
is your body a healthy place to live?
a sacred site? any bitterness inside?
let's strengthen and sweeten ourselves
until that's all there is

when walking in the forest
may i first remove your shoes?

this path to exquisiting can be little
things little food
microscopic gladitudes
pouring purities into our perspectives
until songs of celebration
begin to sing us
to bring us wholly here

amber moon rises from a rock
gazes between shrubs
beaming boldly
obscuring darkness
casting silver silhouettes
moon arrives directly
upon your window sill
and drops in
like blue pools of spilled milk
like welcomed ghosts
wondersome and real

how few
can slip through
the corridors
of illusion
beyond the subways
of thought
between the dominion
of opinions
to stop

.

to stop and see
the sky for what it is
to know for the first time
yet all the time
that we are sitting
in the sky
right now

i look up to my ancestors
and watch their leaves fall

i look for old friends in the night
as they shoot across the sky

i remember my relations
who blossom and erode

and admire steep ancient elders
who stand steadfast in fierce winds

a fire lookout arrives
upon her mountain in the spring time
eager to roam to sing create explore
a few productive weeks pass
before it happens
and it happens at last

one begins to move
in the manner of the neighbors
who happen to be shape-shifting
tai chi masters called clouds

realizing the futility of striving
one begins arriving
assuming cloud-like postures
horizontal freeform nebulous

and on blue days
one simply disappears

heaven has fallen
into the canyon
sunshine-rimmed summits
are streaking the stream
reflecting celestial
cumulous mansions
while juniper's creaking
and glistening abeam

reconsider that deemed impossible
let's investigate established facts
could dads be beams of celestial descent?
mothers star breath heaven sent?
levitation may not pertain to the body
enlightenment is relative
yes thoughts can sustain us
food being merely a supplement
plantbreath our mainstay
are we being consumed by consumerism?
cultures do err
truths have been twisted
greed breeds wars
kindness can cure
this moment is *the* moment
goddess is wild

fly stories

it's easy to just swat it
but wait! a fly has a family!
exclaims a buddhist

that is ridiculous.

meanwhile elsewhere
a fly argues that
some humans *do* have feelings
a human with a heart? ha!

macho flies snort at such absurdities

intimate opportunities

desperately a fly
bzzzz tap bzzz tap
bzzz taps your window glass
stunned and spent
belly up
and still
so easy to kill

with glass in hand you scoop her inside
as you stretch your arm outside

the fly flies away
yet you are closer

intimate opportunities

heaven is a slow pace
abiding where gaps
become graces
where pausing
begets ecstasy
and silence means talking
heaven to heaven

my holiness can not be contained
in a building or a book
the wilder i am, the holier
i am the crag, lone coyote, thunder pine
running like a rush of wind
through the intangible wilderness
i wander
into the invisible landscape
i roam
free of belief
with neither expectations
nor visions nor other burdens
with only wonder
i step up
to the threshold of now

quiet mountain
follows one everywhere
in the marketplace
silence
in the streets
silence
in your heart

sleeping in a beach cave

inside a melody of leaves
the fragrance of your face
fades now into shadows of boughs
where wind slithers invisible
yet perceptible as tears dank and soft
as moss with feathers for fingers
who stretch into tiny dark skies
blind tactile skies newborn skies
leaping crawling somersaulting
stars as if they were glad to be
living on the edge of our cosmos
free to leap adrift beyond pages
to hide behind flickering clouds
above the salt people singing inside
the spray of enraged waves onto
crags of froth and kelp o the
taste of bladderwrack and barnacles…

municipal montanas

in beijing we stroll together
through ancient labyrinth courtyards
amidst sooty weeping willows
and glimpse up
we weave and pause to teeter
atop our clunky cycles
between remnant redbrick hutongs
and peer up
stepping down from buses
climbing up from subways
we see skyward limestone ranges
pale sheer peaks which scatter
toward infinity to summit
as our mountain homes above us
in all directions loom around us
bright-lit ranges know in english
as highrise apartment towers

o savage golden cabbage sun
below green clouds rainbows you've hung
you boogie bad with solar flash
who could resist your hot panache
the mist you've kissed then tumbled some
between white sheets of stratus fun
joy's the way of our big blue house
where none succumb to become a spouse
we clouds are born without a mate
to love we simply saturate

the search for a first-world woe

"what's your problem?" classmates asked
yet she'd no problem that would pass
so in bookshops she'd long look
to learn that there's no problems book

at first she aimed to be a drunk
she'd rove bare-toed with booze undrunk
yet balked at the insinuation
that fun requireth fermentation

she courted next the cancer bane
a slothful painful death-bound lane
though didn't groove ingesting meats
or smokers' clothes which fume for weeks

the search for problems lingered on
long past the first love had begun
with news of infidel it he
one savors one's own company

could this problem-searching flunky
be perchance a drug-crazed junkie?...

... drugs failed however in contrast
with roaming, love and zealous fasts

the perfect problem seemed to be
a welfare mother divorcee
but college profs did quiet insist
join zpg, give kids a miss

globetrotting singles mingle well
with refugees in war-torn hells
with ambassadors and ministers
and amputees come sinister with ceos
a wanderer soon grows

years of third world memories
may prod one toward serenities
of nature, music, solitude
and quiet friends

loneliness is said a loathsome ill
so she now treads a lonesome hill
on high with steep spry granite peaks
she sings she laughs though rarely speaks
except with trees or feathered/furry friends
who frolic at her grateful feet

having skipped across the street
i stood on the sidewalk
and opened your letter
sunlight splashing
a breeze breathed across the page
i read your words
small and concise
yet so kind
so very kind
that they rolled down these cheeks shining
like sunbeams from a thunderhead
like a great meandering delta
converging beneath my chin

we are students of the dark
house called universe
where stars burst from the mist
where winter thrives in moonlit glaciers
we see it all, the eons, the frosts
the auroral obsidian nights
where you were wind
and i water and o
what a storm
what a sacred whirling

i'll suck your leg
mosquito said
or satisfy my fancy
now run around
with a convincing frown
cussing with feet aprancy
so he did the squirm
of the blue glow worm
he tangoed like hungry mice
he rubby-dubbed
tootsies waltzing above
and the neighbors found it nice
though merlin observed
with naught one word
from the jutting of a crag
in the pond below
pollys wagged to and fro
jigging the pollywag
and a swift did sing
a feathering
the windsong phootle-phoot
the javalina report was thundering snort
as they skittled the fluted scoot…

... power lines sang
telephones rang
clocks struck seven past two
the night itself was a merry elf
whence even old snoodle cooed

the man soon slowed
he had stub his toed
which he placed betwixt his teeth

he cried as he stood
in the giggling wood
toe twixt tongue and teeth
i'll zap your knee!
buzz buzz chided she
with her siblings, a choir unseen
the man hopped around
thrumping wobbledly ground
to the commands of the mosquito queen

gentle raindrops
offer opulence
to a suburb-visiting hermit
doors and windows close
tvs begin to glow
and so alas you are alone
with a little sidewalk wilderness
shiver-listening with wet skin
celebrating dipping in
to cloud tears singing softly
in lofty summits of trees
and between raindrops
the stillness
the patient stillness
i swear you can hear
birds listening to it
while trees groove it
yet nobody moves
not even the listening wind

thankfully their monotony
teaches me never to be bored
their dull dazed eyes plead scrutinize
experiment dare pray create
their flaccid flesh says celebrate
aboriginal exercise
their lethargy signs tenderly
abstain from meats and sweets
and packaged treats
and supermarket curiosities
their crumbling posturings convey
the virtues of expanding space
between, if slumping, vertebrae
their tvs encourage me to read
their squabblings not to be in need
of company yet to embrace
cheerfulness humility tenderness sincerity
such excellent teachers these!

life is a kiss
continuous sensual
life is a meal
exquisitely luscious
yes life is a stream
slurping a sip
of the sun
is a source
of all this
life is a storm
showering splattering
colors called canyons and lichens and sky

we are all but dense dreams
and sacred shadows
neither has hell walls
nor heaven a gate
as consumers speak of things
others can be disparaging
each embracing self-perpetuating
facets of the many realms

and you are love
yes, you are love
you who perceives the angelic possibility in all
love walks through walls of doubt
love plants enthusiasm to blossom
in countless hearts throughout
eons of uncertainty
epochs of eternity

as a rainbow contains
all colors beautiful
divine is love, you are radiating
all-embracing, stronger than strength
love shifts stars as if they are marbles
forever abiding in the secret sky of all things
even spirit is a servant of love

active trading in the south pacific

on damp beach sand
i awoke alone
on wild savai'i island*
aside a complex interconnecting
of recent pathways in the sand
the tiny construction had occurred
literally overnight beneath the moon
according to the track marks
a delegation of hundreds of hermit crabs
had convened to the dawn side
of my then-sleeping diaphragm
to swap up shells into their next size
then dispersed before dawn as geometrically and
symmetrically as a thousand radii of an iris
some tracks extending far along the spit
a few vanishing into palm-fringed grasses
most wandering home into the tidal sea
to dine between barnacles and sea stars
as hermit crabs do

*savaii is western samoa's most rugged and paradisical isle

to be a brumby*
is to delight in running
dashing along pebbled beaches
bolting through loamy meadows
as your belly brushes against
the trembling grass
your hooves thunder up black crags
eyes wild with the bliss of freedom
snorting rushing toward the blue
your jagged mane flies
with spirit in it
and your withers have
never ever been held
by a human hand
o to be a brumby!

*a feral free-roaming australian horse

chinese metamorphosis near shangri la

these tribal forest people say they
came from the eggs of a butterfly

in their dialect
with theatrical gesticulations
amidst quiet giggles and hearty imaginations
i attempt to say,

we come from our one shared earth
from the soil who sustains us
rather humbly
so mysteriously
we come from the sun who bestows
on us its favors in
ceaseless songbeam frequencies
from the breeze who breathes rain clouds
eternal farmer swirling wind
who plants seeds in new places
and feathers the sky…

how old am i was not long ago two
remember swimming? as were you
sperm and egg born from another
father sperm and egg mother…

...so i have nothing but narrow notions
to uproot and for now
a meadow in my heart
abrim with gorgeous crooked trees

and you? what does your mind woo?"

make us affluent with forests
of understanding
strengthen us
with hidden virtues
sweeten us
with penetrating silence so
we may be
as lovely
as the afternoon moon
who peers slimly now
from a rift between clouds

women wash aside the river
a toddler squats
slapping glassy water with wide
eyes and fat-padded hands
women sing as silken saris dry
above the sand and stream
coloring the boulders
in the melon morning light
mist rises from the river
to sidle between bending reeds
where ducks waddle and dip
into the dawn

three women at dusk
bathe together
singing and giggling
behind the reeds
innocent moments
celestial scenes these

seasons pass
herenow on the lower colorado
this canoe floats alone
deemed odd by brawny men
who fuel jet boats stoke barbeques
and mow lawns in the desert...

... not a woman seen all week
from my old wooden canoe
drifting by occasional
desert mobile home communities
scattered with their beer cans
along the river

one wonders when
was the last dawn
a woman washed aside this river
her naked toddler squatting
slapping the water with wide
eyes and fat-padded hands
singing

currents swiftly drift this
maple canoe and marveling me
to glide inside mohave reservation
old river broadens and breathes
ducklings zig-paddle, sedges appear
fowl flit and gambol, the water comes clear
so i jump in, all skin and grins
asplash and giggling
new songs of celebration
inside this glade of ancient reeds

thai wild life

wind juggles dust
beneath broad swashing fronds
from deep inside a tropical grove
passing meandering elephants
and a giant, beastly-bright, rainbow iguana
to this market i bring
wild jungle fruits
raising farmers' brows
villagers' suspicions
and astonishment
she is feral they murmur
atavistic heathen
eating savage fruits
scrumptious i insist
blushing they refuse
then a girl pushes
between the sarongs
of her mother and aunt
to accept a fig from the forest

it's precious to travel two-booting
whistlewalking along the rice paddy mounds
balancing between green rice fields
striding straight into the sun
following heartbeats of the earth
into the gloaming
into unknowing
finding new stars
the old friends rearranged

i like to roam beyond the end
of the road
where scant trails are
deep with elephant dung
and leagues beyond
pedestrian hamlets
inside the wild from whence
we all once sprung

an aotea* afternoon

though we said nothing
it's not as if nobody spoke
tuis** twaddled, fantails trilled
rimu trees rasped pleasantries
according to whim
there were oblique gestures of sunlight
and reports by surf and wind
when they whipped
and if they paused
everyone would listen in

*aotea means white cloud in maori and is the
maori name for new zealand's great barrier island
** tuis and fantails are beautiful friendly birds of aotea

i long to be with you at dawn
as our ears first awaken
to silver raindrops singing
upon the roof
to the chubby kettle humming
breathfully then
clearing its voice in a
high-pitched triumphant operetta
to the cactus wrens
flitting excitedly
among dewy junipers
i long to be with you
as our eyes softly open
to sunlight beaming
through cherubic clouds
splashing our lashes
twinklingrinnigathering love
i long to be with you
morning after morning

set sail with me across the sea
on a mokken* sloop for two
with a salacca keel, a bamboo reel
and a pandanus leaf-framed view

let's explore the shores crossing oars
rowing quiet with the tide
and on each isle let's reside awhile
til the jungle vibes confide

why medicine plants and vermillion ants
sing electromagnetically
and how each leaf scribes in relief
thou art magic unto me

* the mokken are gentle roving sea gypsies who lovingly
adopted me in the andaman sea. the mokken are
renowned for their beautiful traditional lifestyle of sailing
and quietly thriving in their humble forest hewn boats
amidst the wild islands of thailand, myanmar and india

christchurch, new zealand

sleeping on my side on the horizon
atop oceanic cliffs
the whole world seems sideways
except for waning hammock moon
slumbering on an old volcano
feels interesting dipping between rocks
which curl around one's torso
to sidle between limbs akimbo

this former forest was flash pasture-ized
all made barren for wool and wood?
tonight leeside this sleeping bag
a solo candle flicker-flags
as if tibetan prayers could flap
pleasing zephyr psalms
this rarest night without a cloud
except for cirrus ribbons blush
and swirl as wisps of nebulae
swells crash beneath the hollowed cliffs
resound around the chest in thuds
through heartrock moonlit godley's head
were you first called godly instead?
wrapped in stars and nightbreath now
your name is understandable

a clock can creep back
into your existence as
you watch your watch and wonder
why you wonder what time it is
who knows what time it is?

it is dark, we are alive
and that's all that matters

night invites the silent in
side darkly walking savoring
without a morsel of attention
toward any timepiece calculation

it is dark, we are alive
and that's all

many so many fear the dark
woods, which is glorious
for the rest of us
who disembark at dusk
to awaken to the universe

god comes to me in taxi stands
in the smile of a child with outstretched hands
she toils with shyness, her eyes avert
then dares "namaste gi" wringing her skirt

through the eyes of a child hush treasures untold
in this girl's soft glance, it's god i behold

god comes to me in a persimmon tree
where old crow cackles and caws
i cackle back to this black-feathered jack
to whose song i render applause

god comes to me in a ridgetop hut
high home to gaddhi shepherds and sheep
glad slapping hands in chapatti lands
with chai and song, then fireside sleep

god comes to me in glacial peaks*
like sets of teeth against the sky
in the rose of dawn my heart is born
om nama shivay

* of the himalaya

the sun doesn't know how strong she is
the moon doesn't know his grace
so how could you know the wonderful skies
hiding behind your face?

first line offerings of *uncivilized ecstasies*

34   the birth of legends, with muddy feet
35   the prophet of profit
36   solitude
37   he embraces me with poetry
38   breathing midstream
39   you come to witness the alpenglow
40   to abide on an alp is
41   he said, you are not grounded enough
42   black-eyed clouds overheard
43   how to access the divine?
44   amber moon rises from a rock
45   how few
46   i look up to my ancestors
47   a fire lookout arrives
48   heaven has fallen
50   reconsider that deemed impossible
50   fly stories
51   intimate opportunities
52   heaven is a slow pace
53   my holiness cannot be contained
54   quiet mountain
55   sleeping in a beach cave
56   municipal montanas
57   o savage golden cabbage sun
58   the search for a first-world woe

60   having skipped across the street
61   we are students of the dark
62   i'll suck your leg
64   gentle raindrops
65   thankfully their monotony
66   life is a kiss
67   we are all but dense dreams
68   active trading in the south pacific
69   to be a brumby
70   chinese metamorphosis near shangri la
72   women wash aside the river
74   thai wild life
75   it's precious to travel two-booting
76   an aotea afternoon
77   i long to be with you at dawn
78   set sail with me across the sea
79   christchurch, new zealand
80   a clock can creep back
81   god comes to me in taxi stands
82   the sun doesn't know

about the author

happy treasures walking the dawn with alpine friends
sipping streams, chasing the wind
bathing beneath waterfalls
whistling words back up to chatty birds
chiming in to wild night animal sing-a-long songs

steeped deep in wonder and dipped in awe
this adventure anthropologist and blissologist
continues to slowly and succulently tour
our one shared home,
this living miracle called earth,
the breathing, loving, fully-feeling being
who is us

"life is so precious
we best proceed slowly
so as not to miss any of it"
— dai adage

if you are fond of this book, you may also enjoy
bliss conscious communication by happy oasis.

feel free to reach the author happy@happyoasis.com

18018578R00051

Made in the USA
San Bernardino, CA
24 December 2014